A Peril o

For Robert & Liz

Thank you *so* much for all your help and expertise over the years. Please see the acknowledgements (p. XI, paragraphs 1 & 2)

Jeremy.

A Peril of the Sea

Jeremy Krikler

Methuen & Co

First published in paperback in Great Britain in 2019 by
Methuen & Co. Ltd.

1

Methuen & Co. Ltd.
Orchard House
Railway Street
Slingsby, York, YO62 4AN
www.methuen.co.uk

Copyright © 2019 Jeremy Krikler
Dr Jeremy Krikler has asserted his moral rights in accordance with the
Copyright, Designs and Patents Act 1988

Methuen & Co Ltd Reg. No. 05278590

ISBN 978 0 413 77836 9
A CIP catalogue record for this title is available from the British Library

Typeset by SX Composing DTP, Rayleigh, Essex

Printed and bound in Great Britain by Clays Ltd., Elcograf S.p.A.

This paperback edition is sold subject to the condition that it shall not,
by way of trade or otherwise be lent, resold, hired out or otherwise
circulated in any form of binding or cover other than that in which it is
published and without a similar condition, including this condition,
being imposed on the subsequent purchaser.

Performance Rights Enquiries: all rights in this play are strictly reserved.
A performance can be staged only once a licence has been issued.
All applications for performance must be submitted to
Methuen & Co Limited [www.methuen.co.uk / rights@methuen.co.uk]
before rehearsals commence.

To

Joe, Mia and Angelica

(*in order of appearance, but equally*)

A Peril of the Sea opened at the Lakeside Theatre, Colchester, and at the Bloomsbury Theatre, London, in December 2017.

Cast (in order of appearance):

Lord Mansfield	Ben Livingstone
Dido Elizabeth Belle	Valerie Isaiah
Commissioning Captain	Ben Livingstone
James Kelsall	Sam Donnelly
'Captain' Zemma Zemma	Valerie Isaiah
Luke Collingwood	Reginald Edwards
First Sailor	Reginald Edwards
Second Sailor	Sam Donnelly

Director	Kate Lovell
Set & Costume Designer	Daisy Blower
Stage Manager	Summer Keeling
Lighting & Sound Manager	Ryan Lester
Sound Effects	Adam McCready

Dramatis Personae

Mansfield William Murray, 1st Earl of Mansfield, Lord Chief Justice in the 1780s

Dido daughter of a slave, niece of and servant to Mansfield (Dido occupies a curious position in the Lord Chief Justice's household: part servant, part member of the family)

Captain slave ship master who appoints Collingwood as captain of the *Zong*

James Kelsall first mate on the *Zong* slave ship

Zemma Zemma African slave merchant

Luke Collingwood surgeon and captain of the *Zong*

First Sailor seaman, experienced in the slave trade

Second Sailor young seaman, inexperienced in the slave trade

Contents

Acknowledgements	xi
A Peril of the Sea	1
Afterword	79

Acknowledgements

I owe a great debt to the University of Essex which nested this work from the start. Department of History funds were crucial to the play's development and staging, and the university-administered Research Impact Acceleration Fund of the ESRC supported it. Theatre specialists at the university – notably, Liz Kuti, Jonathan Lichtenstein and Barbara Peirson – have all left their mark on the play. Help too was provided by the historian Sean Kelley, an accomplished scholar of the slave trade. Sir Sydney Kentridge QC provided guidance on the law. I am grateful, too, for the commentary and suggestions of Joe Krikler, Eliza Kentridge and Vic Gatrell.

Particular thanks go to the director Robert Price of Lubkinfinds Theatre Company, who helped to arrange and direct multiple readings and whose advice on changing aspects of the play was invaluable. Responses of actors as they encountered the play in its various iterations were also helpful in my honing the drama. The final and necessary changes required were identified by the players and the director Kate Lovell as they worked out how best to bring *A Peril of the Sea* to the stage. Daisy Blower, the set and costume designer, did all that could be done with limited resources to transport the audience to a slave ship and a judge's study in London in the eighteenth century. Those responsible for light and sound and for stage management are likewise thanked for their impressive professionalism and work.

Finally, I should note that the quotations from the wills referred to in this play are actual, as is the title of James Park's book on the law of marine insurance which was published in the late-eighteenth century; likewise, the titles of chapters in Park's volume are cited as they appear in his work.

Scene One

Kenwood House, home of **Mansfield**, *the Lord Chief Justice*

[**Mansfield** *sits in his elegant eighteenth-century study, reading and annotating legal papers at his desk. A painting of Countess Mansfield, his late wife, hangs on one of the study walls*]

Mansfield [*calling*] Dido.

Enter **Dido**

Dido Yes, my lord.

Mansfield Dido, my dear, bring my notebooks for the cases of 1779.

Dido Yes, my lord. [*Exit* **Dido**]

[**Mansfield** *continues working*]

Enter **Dido**

[**Dido** *places* **Mansfield**'s *notebooks on his desk and sits down*]

Mansfield Thank you, Dido. [*He leafs through a notebook, looking for a particular case*] What do you think of the Van Loo painting?

Dido A fine likeness, my lord.

Mansfield You don't think I look too serious?

Dido No, no. It reminds me of how I saw you when I was a child. Proud and gentle.

Mansfield A good painting to remember me by?

Dido Don't talk like that, my lord.

Mansfield I grow old, Dido. My work is nearly done.

Dido You make me sad.

Mansfield I remember when you were brought to Kenwood, my dear. How your father worried about you.

Dido You and the countess cared for me.

Mansfield [*looking at the portrait of his late wife*] I miss the countess, Dido, I miss the countess.

Dido I do too, my lord.

Mansfield That love and shrewdness, Dido, it is rare.

Dido I know, my lord.

Mansfield Her fine sense of option, her love of politics. She saw my chances and made me seize them. She makes me strive. [*Pause*] But she is gone. [**Mansfield** *rubs his eyes and then looks at his right hand*] This hand, it aches. That fall from the horse shook the rheumatism out of its slumber, and now it has me.

Dido We must see to your physic, my lord.

Mansfield Physic! What does it do for this hand? [*Pause*] And there is no physic for my heart.

Dido My lord, strive to be happy. The countess would want this. [*Pause*] Theatre, my lord, you need the theatre.

Mansfield No, no. Nothing diverts me. Only work. The law is my refuge.

Dido An uncomfortable refuge, my lord.

Mansfield Uncomfortable?

Dido Hard statutes, implacable precedents, the sword-play of barristers. These do not make for comfort, my lord.

Mansfield What is for some a rack is for me a bed.

Dido What about poetry, my lord? Read some poetry.

Mansfield I do not incline to poetry.

Dido Everybody must incline to poetry, my lord!

Mansfield Not I.

Dido But Alexander Pope is your friend.

Mansfield I like him for his oratory not his poetry. [**Mansfield** *returns to his work, leafing slowly through another case book*] Ah, here it is. [**Mansfield** *studies the case book, and annotates a document on his desk. There is pain in his hands and he must be delicate with them. Without looking up, he gestures at the remaining case books*] Dido, put those back.

Dido What my lord?

Mansfield Take them back to the library.

[*Exit* **Dido**, *swiftly and with some anger, taking the books*]

[**Mansfield** *continues to work. There is the sound of a horse drawing up. A bell rings. Soon, there are sounds of a horse drawing away*]

Enter **Dido**, *holding a package*

Dido Mr. Park has sent to you a manuscript.

Mansfield Good.

Dido These scholars of the law, my lord, must they always bother you? First Blackstone, now Park. Endless discussions. You need more rest.

Mansfield Park needs my final comments.

Dido [*opening the package and taking out the manuscript*] What a grand title. 'System of the Law of Marine Insurances.' Et cetera, et cetera, et cetera. [**Dido** *leafs through the work*] Well, you are cited constantly.

Mansfield I virtually invented that branch of the law.

Dido It sounds dull, my lord.

Mansfield Not at all. Most important. Our islands depend on trade of the seas. And who can trade without knowledge of how insurance can protect them?

Dido Most fascinating.

Mansfield I developed the law of marine insurance into a marvellous clarity. I polished it and polished it, worked away at its flaws and polished some more. Clarity I aimed at and clarity I achieved.

Dido [*laughing*] You do love that word, my lord. And the word 'certainty.' Certainty, certainty, clarity, clarity. When I was a girl and heard you say it, I thought you wanted claret. I expected the footmen to jump to get you drink.

[*They laugh*]

Mansfield Well, Dido, people need clarity. One cannot laugh at that. [*Pause*] The times that people and their lawyers have appeared before me on the basis of confusion is legion. There are lives wasted in pursuit of claims pressed forth on the basis of some imagined precept. I would not have this waste, and so I . . . I clarified.

Dido [*looking at the manuscript's table of contents*] What extraordinary chapters!

Mansfield What?

Dido Listen. 'Of The Policy,' 'Of The Construction of the Policy.'

Mansfield Well?

Dido [*dramatically*] 'Of Losses by Capture and Detention of Princes.' [*With mock desperation*] 'Of Abandonment.'

Mansfield Dido, do not mock. Park's categories are appropriate. I helped frame them. You've no idea what we are up against.

Dido My lord?

Mansfield An army of underwriters! They are great wrigglers.

Dido Wrigglers, my lord?

Mansfield Oh yes, Dido. Wrigglers. They do all to wriggle out of a claim for insurance. Counsel for a wriggling underwriter has frequently come before me. But my judgements are hooks on which they may writhe but off which they cannot wriggle. And then they pay. Park's book will help in the war against the wrigglers.

Dido What of this chapter? 'Of Losses by the Barratry of the Master or Mariners.' Barratry?

Mansfield What of it?

Dido It sounds rude, my lord.

Mansfield Rude?

Dido What is barratry?

Mansfield Fraud.

Dido Oh. And then there is the chapter 'Of Losses by . . .' [*Pause*]

Mansfield [*laughing*] Yes?

Dido [*in mock terror*] 'Perils of the Sea.'

Mansfield I would not joke about that Dido. The ocean is often a peril to the lives of those on it. Storms, calms, privateers, pirates, men o' war, shoals, sharks. The rats scrape at the puncheons of water and the casks of salted meat. The ship's belly crawls with rodents. And all around is the vast, heaving and indifferent ocean. And most of the sailors, they cannot swim.

Dido [*still leafing through the book*] I like the names of the ships.

Mansfield Oh, yes?

Dido The *Sally*, the *Joke*, the *Bonny*, the *Calibar*, the *New Calibar*, the *Prospero*. Here's a good one. The *Zong*. And what of this? The . . .

Mansfield [*suddenly concerned*] Let me see the manuscript.

Dido What is it, my lord?

Mansfield Let me see the work. Give me the manuscript. [**Dido**, *puzzled, hands the work to him*] Dido, have one of the footmen bring me port.

Dido Yes, my lord. [*Exit* **Dido**

[**Mansfield** *begins to study the manuscript. After a while, he finds what he is looking for and reads intently*]

Mansfield The *Zong*. [*Pause*] The *Zong*.

[*Sounds of the sea – faint at first – become clearer*]

Scene Two

The Captain's cabin on a slave ship

[*The* **Captain** *is reading a letter. With him is* **James Kelsall**, *one of the ship's officers*]

Captain [*slapping his neck*] This wretched coast. Why must we pick up mosquitoes as well as slaves?

Kelsall This is the worst season, sir.

Captain I've got instructions here from Liverpool to arrange a second ship and cargo for Jamaica.

Kelsall A second one, sir?

Captain Yes. The *Zong*. The prize taken off the Dutch.

Kelsall Will we leave together with it, sir?

Captain No, no. This ship's nearly full. The *Zong* needs a full cargo. That takes time. I want you to be on that ship, Kelsall.

Kelsall [*hopefully*] Am I to be the Captain, sir?

Captain I'd thought of Collingwood.

Kelsall But he's a surgeon, sir.

Captain You think you'd do a better job?

Kelsall I have more skills of the sea, sir. [*Pause*] He knows little of navigation.

Captain He knows enough. Anyway, you can help him. You could be first mate.

Kelsall But, sir . . .

Captain Kelsall, the *Zong* needs a Captain who knows how to buy slaves. What do you know about that?

Kelsall [*resentfully*] I have been present at the purchases, sir.

Captain That's not the same as inspecting, choosing. It's an art. Nobody does it better than Collingwood. Many times he's saved us from low prices in Jamaica. Or worse. You've seen him at his work.

Kelsall I have, sir.

Captain The thoroughness. Nothing escapes him. Everything scrutinised. Their gums, their eyes, their every crease.

Kelsall I have seen slaves chosen and bought, sir.

Captain The yaws, the flux, the scurvy, the gonorrhoea, he will find the slightest trace. He won't have disease on board. [*Pause*] You can't do that Kelsall. You can't stock a slaver. [*Pause*] Is our cooper well yet?

Kelsall Not quite, sir.

Captain Damn that! I must have the water butts filled and checked.

Kelsall The African cooper trims the puncheons, sir.

Captain Good. Nothing worse than leaky puncheons on a voyage. [*Pause*] Ever been on a voyage when the sweet water's run out, and all you've got is sips of the sour?

Kelsall No, sir.

Captain The torture of it. [*Pause*] You dream of streams, of goblets of clear, cool water, but you wake with a tongue of wood. And the undrinkable ocean all around you. [*Pause*] I would speak with the surgeon. Call Collingwood.

[*Exit* **Kelsall**

[*The* **Captain** *reads the instructions relating to the* Zong]

Enter **Kelsall**

Captain I asked you to fetch the surgeon.

Kelsall Sir, Zemma Zemma is here.

Captain [*alarmed*] Zemma Zemma?

Kelsall Yes, sir. On board ship. Brought by canoe from Anomabu.

Captain Bring the merchant down at once.

Kelsall Yes, sir. [**Kelsall** *makes to leave*]

Captain Oh, Kelsall.

Kelsall Sir.

Captain Be sure to address Zemma Zemma as *Captain* Zemma Zemma.

Kelsall Yes, sir. [*Exit* **Kelsall**

[*The* **Captain** *draws out a bottle of rum and two goblets and waits with some nervousness. After a short while, there is a knock*]

Captain Yes.

[*The door opens*]

Enter **Kelsall**

Kelsall Sir, Captain Zemma Zemma is here.

Enter **Zemma Zemma**, *an African slave trader*

[*The* **Captain** *moves to shake his hand*]

Captain Captain Zemma Zemma, my dear friend! [**Zemma Zemma** *ignores the proffered hand. The* **Captain** *turns to* **Kelsall**] Let us be alone.

Kelsall Sir. [*Exit* **Kelsall**

Zemma Zemma Your men give me trouble. Why?

Captain This was an error, my dear Captain Zemma Zemma, an error.

Zemma Zemma Error?

Captain When your sons brought the captives on board the ship, some of my sailors . . .

Zemma Zemma Damn your sailors. They think my sons are slaves?

Captain It was an error, Captain.

Zemma Zemma Why they think my sons are slaves?

Captain Captain Zemma Zemma, this will never happen again, I . . .

Zemma Zemma Your men think when they see black skin, they see slaves. Do I look like a slave to you?

Captain Of course not.

Zemma Zemma Of course not?

Captain Of course not.

Zemma Zemma Of course not, what?

Captain Of course not, Captain Zemma Zemma.

[**Zemma Zemma** *sits down at the* **Captain**'s *table without being asked. The* **Captain** *joins him*]

Captain Would you like some rum?

[**Zemma Zemma** *answers by patting the table with an open palm. The* **Captain** *pours rum into goblets and passes one to*

[Zemma Zemma *who raises it, looks into it, measuring with his eye how much rum has been poured. Without drinking, he sets the goblet down and pushes it towards the* **Captain**. *The* **Captain** *pours more rum and passes the goblet back to* **Zemma Zemma** *who drinks in silence*]

Zemma Zemma If this ship brings trouble again, we will choke your supplies. No canoes. No slaves. No yams. No water. You understand?

Captain Yes, yes, Captain Zemma Zemma. There will be no more trouble, I assure you.

Zemma Zemma Good. Now make good. [*The* **Captain** *pours more rum.* **Zemma Zemma** *gulps it down and puts the goblet on the table*] Make good. [*The* **Captain** *makes to pour but* **Zemma Zemma** *stops him*] No more rum. I want goods.

Captain Goods?

Zemma Zemma Goods.

Captain I don't understand.

Zemma Zemma What do I exchange slaves for?

Captain Why the usual, my good Captain – metal goods, firearms, cloth.

Zemma Zemma That's right. I want them. [*The* **Captain** *is puzzled*] Your men held my sons as slaves. You must give me goods for them.

Captain We released your sons as soon as we realised the error. We sent a bottle of finest rum to you at Anomabu. We apologised to them. We . . .

Zemma Zemma Make good or you don't trade here. [*Pause*] Ever.

[*A long pause*]

Captain What will you have, good Captain Zemma Zemma?

Zemma Zemma Knives and guns and cloth. Two slaves' worth.

Captain All right.

Zemma Zemma [*getting up*] Good.

Captain [*rising*] Will you help me stock a second ship?

Zemma Zemma When I get back.

Captain Back? You go into the interior.

Zemma Zemma Yes.

Captain Oh. Well, Captain Zemma Zemma, I shall arrange for goods to be brought on deck.

Zemma Zemma You come up soon. My canoe waits. [*Pause*] Guns, knives, cloth. For two slaves.

[*Exit* **Zemma Zemma**

[*The* **Captain** *ruminates*]

Enter **Collingwood**

Captain Ah, Dr. Collingwood, you're back from Anomabu Fort. Please, sit. Rum?

Collingwood Yes, sir. Thank you. [**Collingwood** *drinks*]

Captain Good?

Collingwood Very good, sir.

[*They sip their rum*]

Captain We've been in this wretched trade a long time, Collingwood. [*Pause*] The Lord snatches you away if you stay in it too long.

Collingwood I know what slave ships incubate, sir.

Captain [*slapping at another mosquito*] And this damn African coast as well! [*Pause*] The ways of the Lord we cannot fathom, especially in this trade.

Collingwood I did not know that the Lord would make me a surgeon to serve the trade. I had hoped for a different station, sir.

Captain What was that?

Collingwood To heal the sick somewhere in England. I could not get a position.

Captain I wanted a life in the Royal Navy. It was not God's will.

Collingwood The Lord must have put us here for some purpose, sir.

Captain Yes.

Collingwood When I was in England last, sir, I read a treatise that God created the trade to save the African captives.

Captain Yes?

Collingwood That God uses us to buy the captives so that the African merchants will not put them to death.

Captain Well, I have known of captives who were starved if not sold to us. Or beheaded.

Collingwood At New Calibar. I'll never forget that, sir.

[*They drink*]

Captain How many behind the barricado now?

Collingwood Four hundred and three, sir.

Captain We'll have to stow them belowdecks and set off soon. Once the butts are filled with fresh water we must get away. I don't like staying on this coast longer than I need to. It's a pestilence. [*The* **Captain** s*laps his neck again*]

Collingwood Another died this morning. A man boy.

Captain Damn! Of what?

Collingwood Of chagrin. He stopped taking food. We did everything to lever the mouth. To no avail.

[*Pause*]

Captain Collingwood?

Collingwood Sir.

Captain Wouldn't you like to be a Captain, Collingwood?

Collingwood [*with deference and surprise*] I'm the ship's surgeon, sir, and content with that.

Captain You don't want to be Master of a slave ship?

Collingwood Well, sir, I have sometimes had ambition to . . .

Captain Twenty shillings more each month.

Collingwood I have never complained of my remuneration, sir, and . . .

Captain Some tribute slaves thrown into the bargain that you can sell on your own account.

Collingwood Sir, I . . .

Captain A commission on the total number sold.

Collingwood That is *your* right, sir, not mine.

Captain Just get the black cattle to Jamaica with no more than the usual losses. Our backers balk at more than five, at most ten percent wastage.

Collingwood I don't understand, sir. You're the Captain.

Captain [*picking up the document he had been reading earlier*] I have an opportunity in my hand. Will you grasp it? Our masters in Liverpool have given instructions regarding the *Zong*.

Collingwood The Dutch slave ship, sir?

Captain Yes, yes. She's ours now, bought for a song. If the Dutch are stupid enough to send ships to these waters, our privateers will snap them up like sharks do dead slaves. The *Zong*'s half-packed with negroes. We need someone to pack her full and sail her to Jamaica.

Collingwood How many slaves on board the *Zong* now, sir?

Captain Two hundred, I'm told.

Collingwood She's a small slaver, sir. She looks but a hundred ton.

Captain They want her tight-packed. We have goods enough to trade for another two hundred and fifty.

Collingwood Four hundred and fifty slaves in that ship!

Captain Collingwood, you're a fine surgeon. You'll keep wastage low.

Collingwood Well, sir, I keep wastage low by selecting carefully.

Captain That I know.

Collingwood To establish price or suitability of Africans for the trade might be a strange use of physic, sir, but I do it, I believe, well.

Captain Excellently well.

[*A brief silence*]

Collingwood I've never captained a vessel, sir.

Captain Come, Collingwood. How many slaving voyages have you done?

Collingwood Ten, sir. But navigation is not my forte. Jamaica is far and . . .

Captain Kelsall can help you. He'll go as first mate. I've already spoken to him. [*Getting up, he rolls out a map on a table*] Look. Once you've got your slaves in Anomabu, sail for Saint Thomas. Replenish there. Then cut across the belly of the Atlantic to Jamaica and make your killing. Stop at Barbados if you need to. [*Pause*] Keep them well chained and watch out for insurrection, especially in the early part of the voyage.

Collingwood That I know, sir.

Captain On one voyage, the unchained African wenches passed a file to the men and rebellion nearly overwhelmed the ship. We had to keep the swivel guns blasting. The cost of it! We killed forty prime slaves. Forty prime! You know what they would have fetched in Jamaica.

Collingwood A great loss, sir.

Captain And our merchants had no insurance against insurrection! Only God saved us from the rebellion. We gave prayerful thanks.

Collingwood God has saved us many times on the seas.

Captain Many times. [*Pause*] Collingwood, you're the man for this job. It will make you. Our masters in Liverpool will get two cargoes instead of one. Nine hundred slaves at thirty pounds a head. A huge profit. We'll come back heroes, I in this ship, you in the *Zong*. What say Collingwood?

Collingwood It tempts, sir.

Captain We could put our earnings towards a slaving voyage of our own.

Collingwood We do know the trade, sir.

Captain We'd be done with this African coast. Wouldn't it be grand to sit in Liverpool and send others out for us?

Collingwood Grand, sir. Yes.

Captain This will make your fortune and your reputation. Captain Luke Collingwood, Master of the *Zong*!

[*Blackout*

Scene Three

Kenwood House – the study

[**Mansfield** *is alone, working on a document*]

Enter **Dido**

Mansfield Write Mr Park a note of thanks for the manuscript.

Dido Of course, my lord. [**Dido** *makes to leave*]

Mansfield Oh, Dido.

Dido Yes, my lord.

Mansfield Tell Park I will write to him soon about certain matters.

Dido Is there anything else, my lord?

Mansfield No, no. Where have you been, my dear?

Dido At the dairy.

Mansfield The dairy. [*Pause*] The countess used to spend so much time there. So proud of the butter we produced. All is in order?

Dido Yes, my lord.

Mansfield The livestock healthful?

Dido Mostly, my lord?

Mansfield Mostly?

Dido Molly continues to weaken.

Mansfield She was the countess's favourite cow.

Dido She is attended to, my lord.

Mansfield Good. Your superintendence of the dairy is superb.

Dido I have a good staff.

[*A silence*]

Mansfield You have been a long time at the dairy.

Dido I was also walking the grounds, my lord. I . . . [*Pause*]

Mansfield What is it, Dido? What's the matter? [**Dido** *does not answer*] What troubles you, dear child?

Dido No matter, my lord.

Mansfield Tell me, Dido?

Dido The committees of Parliament.

Mansfield Yes?

Dido The committees into the slave trade, my lord.

Mansfield [*tenderly*] Don't read what distresses you.

Dido [*distressed*] That slave on the ship cast down, refusing food, whipped and then by chance to see his sister brought aboard. To look upon her, to weep, to be unable to speak. [*Pause*] How can England be party to this?

Mansfield The times change, Dido. This trade will end, I am sure.

Dido You cannot end it, my lord? You are the Lord Chief Justice.

Mansfield Dido, what comes before me pertains hardly to the area of liberty. It is the world of property and commerce upon which I sit in judgement. To identify and set the rules for transaction and recompense – that is my focus. The slaves have come but little into that. I have done what I could for them.

Dido What you could, my lord?

Mansfield I have ruled against a master's unlawful imprisonment of a slave.

Dido Oh, Somersett.

Mansfield I have used technicality to free another.

Dido One slave! One slave, my lord, when our ships carry myriads from Africa for sale. You release one slave while a million are lashed to labour in our colonies.

Mansfield I have done what I could, Dido. The law ties my hands.

Dido [*pause*] My lord, the trade in people is . . . it is so . . . strange.

Mansfield It is an abomination, but it exists and I am forced to subject it to the rules of all commerce.

Dido But people . . .

Mansfield [*pleading*] Dido, Dido, property is property and cannot escape the law. That is what Parliament and the courts decree. And I cannot escape the law. It pains me.

Dido It pains *you*, my lord. The slaves, the people from whom I came . . .

Mansfield Dido, within the laws governing property, I do all that I can for the slaves.

Dido [*pause*] It is only by an accident, my lord, by the . . . the kindness of my . . . my father, the man who would not allow me or my mother into his household, that I was not the subject of a frenzied purchase in the market of some colony.

Mansfield Dido, Dido, stop this cruelty to yourself.

Dido This island sits in an ocean of cruelty. You are the Lord Chief Justice. Dry up that ocean, my lord.

Mansfield Dido, Dido. *I* cannot rule for emancipation of the slaves. That is for Parliament. The law in this country, in all civilized countries, makes property sacred. I cannot interfere with its order, or everything is unravelled.

Dido What then is the use of your work, my lord?

Mansfield The use of my work? What is the use of my work? [*Pause*] Do you know how oppressive the law can be when it is confused?

Dido What of it, my lord?

Mansfield Lives can be spent wandering in a maze of the law.

Dido The law, the law, the law, my lord. Is there nothing higher than this?

Mansfield Dido, I have seen people broken, losing all they have, because contradictions in the law misled them into false hope. My life's work has been to make the law certain.

Dido If the law is made clear but remains cruel what . . .

Mansfield Dido! When I took over as Chief Justice, the law, the law of commerce, was a winding, convoluted thing. Nobody, nobody could follow it. I tracked it down. I looked for contradiction and eliminated it. I hunted for uncertainty and dissolved it.

Dido Uncertainty. The enemy.

Mansfield Yes. The enemy. The tangled mess I found I untangled, I cut away what would prevent the flowering of the law of commerce in this great age of trade.

Dido Trade. How I have come to hate that word.

Mansfield [*sternly*] This country is made great by its commerce. My work has allowed this. Whoever engages in trade, no matter what it be, knows where he stands. Where others have sown confusion, I have provided direction. It has been my life's work, my life's work. The countess herself has . . . [**Mansfield**'s *voice breaks and he looks at Lady Mansfield's portrait*]

Dido Oh, my lord, do not grieve so.

Mansfield [*getting up from his chair, walking to his wife's portrait and speaking to it*] My darling. [**Mansfield** *falls silent*]

Dido [*pointing to the papers on his desk, trying to distract him from his grief*] What is it you work at, my lord?

Mansfield What?

Dido This work, my lord?

Mansfield Oh. I discourse upon Park's manuscript.

Dido You are writing to him, my lord?

Mansfield Yes. The subjects are complex. [*Pause*] I should continue my work.

Dido Yes, my lord.

Mansfield I will have the door closed. I must read out my letter to Mr. Park. [*Pause.* **Mansfield**'s *spirit lifts as he recalls*] My dear friend Alexander Pope taught me always to read out what one writes. One never knows how words are received until they are uttered.

Dido [*laughing*] I have seen you acting your judgements before the mirror, my lord.

Mansfield Well, no mirror this time. Just ear.

[*Exit* **Dido**, *closing the door*

Mansfield [*perusing his letter to Park and then, standing, beginning to read aloud*] Dear Mr. Park, it was with pleasure . . . [**Mansfield** *murmurs briefly and then puts up his finger*] Ah, here we are. [*He begins to orate, as if before an audience*] Under the law of marine insurance, and subject to the contract, there can be claim to underwriters for slaves who die at sea. For example, for slaves killed when an insurrection is put down. The contract will never cover slaves who die of disease or suicide, including by self-starvation, of which there is much. These are established features of the trade, quite natural to it, called – I believe – the 'wastage.' If the voyage is subject to a peril of the sea . . . [*There is a knock at the door*]

Enter **Dido**

Mansfield Yes?

Dido My lord, we have forgotten your physic.

Mansfield Oh, yes. Can't this wait?

Dido Your physician says no, my lord.

Mansfield Ruled by physicians. I will come in a few minutes.

Dido Good, my lord. [*Pause*] You are back with 'perils of the sea,' my lord?

Mansfield What?

Dido When I entered, your discourse was on perils of the sea.

Mansfield Oh, yes. I am writing to Mr. Park about the circumstances when sl . . . [**Mansfield** *catches himself*]

Dido What my lord?

Mansfield The circumstances when cargo can be jettisoned and claimed for under a contract of insurance.

Dido What? Dispense with the cargo and claim for it?

Mansfield Oh, yes, Dido. Sometimes, a peril of the sea, some act of God, can make this an absolute necessity. Not to throw the cargo overboard can endanger the whole voyage and the crew.

Dido How so?

Mansfield Well . . . [*Pause*]

Dido How so, my lord?

Mansfield Well, let us say that an enemy engaged the ship.

Dido Yes?

Mansfield And the ship escaped but was damaged, so that water began to enter it.

Dido I see.

Mansfield The crew could jettison cargo to raise the damaged parts clear above the waves.

Dido And then they could claim on the cargo cast overboard?

Mansfield Yes.

Dido Ingenious, my lord.

Mansfield Indeed. The law has wrapped itself tight about insurance and the sea. I have seen to that.

Dido Congratulations, my lord.

Mansfield Do not tease me, child. I would finish my correspondence with Park. Please close the door. [**Dido** *makes to leave*] Oh, Dido.

Dido Yes, my lord.

Mansfield Send to town for one of my clerks. I will have a clean copy of my response to Park, and I will retain the draft.

Dido I can do the copy for you, my lord.

Mansfield No, no.

Dido I am always writing for you, my lord. My hand is fairer than yours, and your affliction . . .

Mansfield No, no, Dido. Not this letter. I will have a clerk.

[*Exit* **Dido**, *puzzled, closing the door*

Mansfield [*perusing the draft of his letter, adding a few phrases by hand and murmuring until he finds the point in his letter that he had not read out. He orates*] To consider slaves as if they were livestock is shocking. But the judge must rise above what shocks and keep the law clear. Now, to elucidate further what may fall under the category 'perils of the sea,' I would direct you to the following judgements . . . [**Mansfield** *walks to and fro, thinking, while the sound of the ocean, faint at first, gets louder*] Judgements relating to perils of the sea . . . perils of the sea . . . [**Mansfield** *stops by his wife's portrait and speaks to it*] The sea, my love . . . the sea becomes more important to me. I am bound up with it in some way. So fearsome, but something draws me to it.

[*Blackout*

Scene Four

The Zong – *in darkness*

[*Sounds of the sea, cracking of a whip, people shuffling, chains clinking, sounds of distress, fear*]

Sailor [*offstage, cursing*] Get in there, you black bastards.

[*Sounds of slamming and locking, sailors walking across the deck*]

Stage lights up

[*Part of a huge wooden barrier, running across the breadth of the ship, can be seen. Ten feet high, this is the barricado, behind which slaves are kept on a slaver when on deck. It is not possible to see behind the barricado but the sounds of the captives clamouring in more than one of the West African languages – Igbo, Fante – together with the sound of an infant crying can be heard*]

Enter **Captain Luke Collingwood** *with* **Kelsall**,
the first mate

Collingwood Oy.

Sailors [*offstage, calling*] Sir.

Collingwood Did you use the whip on the three I bought?

First Sailor [*offstage*] Only on the deck, sir. To frighten the niggers. They was movin' too slow, sir.

Collingwood Good. I'm the Master of the *Zong* and flesh will be stroked by the cat only when required. I don't want unnecessary cuts. Infections are the enemy of price. Watch what you do.

Sailors [*offstage*] Sir.

Collingwood [*to* **Kelsall**] I haven't worked ten years as a ship's surgeon not to know how to deliver the cargo in good order. You inflict punishment when absolutely necessary, and grade it according to offence. Refusing to eat is not the same as insurrection. Ill usage for no purpose leads, at worst, to wastage; at best, to blemishes which lead the purchasers in the West Indies to niggle over price, drive it down. The best slave is scarless, well-nourished, shiny. [*Pause*] Kelsall.

Kelsall Sir

Collingwood We want stocks of palm oil adequate to buff the negroes when we get to market. I learned that trick from the African traders. You learn a lot from them. [**Kelsall** *nods.* **Collingwood** *and* **Kelsall** *walk over to the barricado*] This is a fine barricado.

Kelsall They are too pressed behind it, sir.

Collingwood The *Zong* is not a large ship. [*Inspecting the barricado*] This is well constructed.

Kelsall Slaves won't escape from there, especially with those guards.

[**Kelsall** *points up to some sailors who are not visible to the audience. The sailors would be positioned on a platform that runs high up against the side of the barricado, leaning against the top of the barricado, with weaponry trained on the slaves on the other side of it*]

Collingwood [*shouting*] Keep those guns pointing over 'em. Yes. Good. That's right. [*Gesturing at two cannons thrust into apertures cut into the barricado*] These are loaded?

Kelsall Yes, sir.

Collingwood With small shot?

Kelsall Yes, sir.

Collingwood Good. [*Pause*] How many slaves on board now?

Kelsall Four hundred and thirty-seven.

Collingwood Can we take more?

Kelsall We're short of crew. This is a small ship, sir.

Collingwood We could take five more slaves.

Kelsall There's a canoe load set to come from shore for inspection, sir. [*Pointing*] Look, sir, it's coming in.

[**Collingwood** *joins* **Kelsall** *in watching the canoe as it draws closer to the ship*]

Collingwood Good Lord, they know how to move those canoes. Stab, stab, stab at the water.

Kelsall They should teach our sailors how to do it.

Collingwood Do you remember the canoes at New Calibar?

Kelsall The time we came in, sir, and the black traders hadn't seen slavers for a while?

Collingwood That's right. Canoes appeared from everywhere carrying the captives to us. Like a school of giant fish.

Kelsall We've never stocked up so quickly.

Collingwood Prices were good.

Kelsall They were indeed, sir.

Collingwood [*shaking his head*] But the Captain's frenzied purchase didn't leave me time to inspect the slaves properly.

Kelsall I remember, sir.

Collingwood By the time we got to Jamaica, a lot had died. Others were deathly ill.

Kelsall I remember.

Collingwood One in five was refuse! Sold for a pittance. [*Pause*] Kelsall, I prefer to make a thorough examination of the captives before buying. It's the most useful work a surgeon can do for a slaver. The Captain at New Calibar wouldn't let me to do my work. He was a shark. Taking slaves too quickly. Here, I'm the Captain and the surgeon. I decide. [*Pause*] They'll be here in a minute. [*Looking through a telescope*] It's Zemma Zemma! Look. [*Passing the telescope to* **Kelsall**] The man sitting by the guards.

Kelsall [*looking through the telescope*] Yes, sir. It's him. Captain Zemma Zemma!

Collingwood We've got to keep that black trader sweet. Fetch me a bottle of wine.

[*Exit* **Kelsall**

[**Collingwood** *looks at the canoe drawing closer and waves*]

Enter **Kelsall**, *giving* **Collingwood** *the wine*

Collingwood [*looking at the bottle*] This isn't good enough.

Kelsall Not good enough, sir?

Collingwood Zemma Zemma is most particular. Get me the best wine.

Kelsall Sir. [*Exit* **Kelsall**

[**Collingwood** *continues to look out at the approaching canoe*]

Enter **Kelsall**, *handing* **Collingwood** *a different bottle of wine*

Collingwood This should do.

Kelsall They're here! Oy, you sailors, help Captain Zemma Zemma aboard! [*Sounds of a man being helped aboard can be heard*]

Enter '**Captain**' **Zemma Zemma**

Collingwood Captain Zemma Zemma! An honour to see you again.

Zemma Zemma Where's the captain?

Collingwood I'm the captain.

Zemma Zemma You not the doctor?

Collingwood I'm the surgeon and the captain.

Zemma Zemma You can make trade?

Collingwood Yes indeed.

Zemma Zemma You have guns and cloth?

Collingwood Yes. Excellent guns and cloth.

Zemma Zemma Good.

Collingwood I have something for you. [**Collingwood** *hands over a bottle of wine*]

Zemma Zemma [*disapprovingly*] No rum?

Collingwood We can get you a bottle of that, too. [*To* **Kelsall**] Get some rum for Captain Zemma Zemma.

[*Exit* **Kelsall**

Collingwood How is your family?

Zemma Zemma You met my family?

Collingwood No. Some of the Captains I worked with did.

Zemma Zemma How's your family?

Collingwood Oh, fine, fine!

Zemma Zemma Good.

Collingwood What do you have for us, Zem... eh, Captain Zemma Zemma?

Zemma Zemma I have ten. Four males.

Enter **Kelsall**, *with a bottle of rum which he passes to* **Collingwood**

Collingwood [*offering the bottle to his guest*] For you, Captain Zemma Zemma.

Zemma Zemma [*uncorking the bottle and taking a swig*] Good.

Collingwood Can I view the men first?

Zemma Zemma [*loudly, in Fante*] Up, up, up!

[*The sound of people being brought aboard the ship can be heard*]

Collingwood One at a time, please. I'll view one at a time.

[**Zemma Zemma** *gestures for the first slave to be brought before* **Collingwood**. *The sound of a slave being shoved forward can be heard – the audience cannot see the slave*]

Collingwood [*beginning his inspection*] He's sickly. Yellow eyes, bleeding gums. Too old. Not him.

[**Zemma Zemma** *stares silently in the direction of the old captive, then, in an offhand manner, points at him and signals his fate by making a chopping motion with his hands; he beckons another slave forward.* **Collingwood** *looks at the slave – the audience cannot see the slave but the inspection can be heard*]

Collingwood [*inspecting the slave*] Yes, open that mouth. Good teeth and gums. No infections in the throat. Eyes clear. [*A slapping can be heard as* **Collingwood** *walks round the slave*] Good musculature. [*Returning to* **Zemma Zemma**] Can you make him jump? [**Zemma Zemma** *gestures towards the slave – the sound of jumping can be heard*] He'll do. If we find nothing once he's stripped. I want a full examination. Tell the others to strip. And then bring the females up.

Zemma Zemma Wait. I want to see goods.

Collingwood Of course, Captain Zemma Zemma. Come to my cabin and we can have rum while the wares are brought up.

Zemma Zemma Guns and cloth only.

Collingwood Of course.

[*Blackout*

Scene Five

The Zong *– on deck*

[**Collingwood** *is looking out to shore. Sounds of someone boarding the vessel can be heard*]

Enter **Kelsall**

Collingwood How is Anomabu?

Kelsall Good, sir, good. I have arranged for purchase of the victuals.

Collingwood Excellent.

Kelsall Sir, the Governor of Anomabu Fort . . .

Collingwood Stubbs?

Kelsall Yes, sir, Mr. Stubbs.

Collingwood What?

Kelsall He sends his congratulations on your commission, sir.

Collingwood That is kind.

Kelsall He asked, sir, if you would also be acting as surgeon on this voyage?

Collingwood Of course, I shall.

Kelsall [*slyly*] He says the crew has luck, sir. You're an experienced surgeon.

Collingwood [*defensively*] I know the sea, too. I have gone from here to the West Indies near a dozen times.

Kelsall Of course, sir. [*Pause*] There is a request from the Governor, sir.

Collingwood Yes? What does he want?

Kelsall His time here is over. He wants passage home.

Collingwood There will be no free passage on the *Zong* except for sailors and negroes. Crew and cargo only. That's my rule. All others pay.

Kelsall He will pay, sir. The usual rate. He begs to bring four slaves with him for sale in Jamaica.

Collingwood Am I to feed and physic them at my expense?

Kelsall No, no, sir. He will pay something for the inconvenience.

Collingwood Something? Why, I may ask for one of the slaves. Can we accommodate more cargo?

Kelsall We are tight-packed on this small ship, sir. And short of crew.

Collingwood Well. It's only four slaves. No more than four?

Kelsall No, sir.

Collingwood I suppose we can adjust a few legs and arms to squeeze them in. [*They laugh*] Are you sorry to be leaving Anomabu, Kelsall?

Kelsall No. This coast takes its vengeance on the white man if he stays too long. [*Pause*] It takes its vengeance on the black man, too.

Collingwood What?

Kelsall The slaves we don't buy. That old man you rejected was made headless.

Collingwood [*pause*] I will not buy those whom I cannot sell.

Kelsall That is the first law of our trade.

Collingwood The African merchants are not under my command. Disease, age, weakness – these I cannot take aboard the ship. The merchants should not bring them to me. I choose only those fit for the trade. It is not a calculus I enjoy.

Kelsall The African traders have their calculus too, sir, and ours twines about theirs. If they cannot find another buyer amongst the ships or the Africans, they have no use for the captives.

Collingwood I know this, and it is diabolical, but it is not on my head. Each slave I take I consider my responsibility – to feed, to heal if sick . . . .

Kelsall To bring to market in Jamaica.

Collingwood Yes, to bring to market in Jamaica.

Kelsall What a maw that island has for slaves!

Collingwood It is a maw that feeds us.

Kelsall It does indeed, sir.

[*They fall silent*]

Collingwood [*shaking his head, as if in wonder*] The alchemy of it all!

Kelsall Alchemy, sir?

Collingwood The alchemy by which we stock a cargo for Jamaica . . . . . .Do you know, Kelsall, there are times when I look at what we've brought from England – metals and guns and cloths and knives. I go into the hold and I take some of them out. I hold them in my hands.

Kelsall Sir?

Collingwood And I look upon the goods and I feel them, and I ask myself . . . what power transforms these goods into flesh? One moment, it is cloth and metals and guns and knives. And the next, it is, it is . . . people!

Kelsall [*laughing*] We make goods into souls, sir.

Collingwood Yes. Goods into souls. [*Pause*] Well, let's toast our full cargo. Rum?

Kelsall A wonderful idea, sir.

[*Exit* **Collingwood** *and* **Kelsall**, *walking off*

[*Blackout*

Scene Six

The Zong – *on deck*

[**First Sailor** *and* **Second Sailor** *close and secure a grate which leads down to the belowdecks where the slaves are held, chained*]

First Sailor That's the last few chained.

Second Sailor Tight down there. Like spoons.

First Sailor We can get 'em up in shifts once we've set off.

Second Sailor Hot down there.

First Sailor How many voyages you been on in the trade?

Second Sailor This is my first.

First Sailor Well, belowdecks gets warm. Gets hot. I been on voyages where steam comes out the grating. Like there's a fire belowdecks. When we went down, it was like we was in their lungs. They was gasping and our clothes was dripping. The sound of that breathing! You don't forget it. A wind moaning in the belly of the ship. First voyage in the trade, you say?

Second Sailor Yes.

First Sailor You never forget your first voyage in this trade.

Second Sailor No?

First Sailor No. I was a fresh boy like you once. First time you see a whipping or some slave forced to eat, you'll be shocked. Then you see it again. And again. You expect it. It don't shock you no more. Something else does. Then you see that. Again and again. Then that don't shock you. My advice. Whenever you see something that shocks, know that you'll see that again and again and it won't shock. It don't take long. The trade schools you quick. Knocks the shock out of you.

Second Sailor You still get shocked in the trade?

First Sailor Every voyage shocks. In some new way. For a time. On my last voyage . . .

Second Sailor Yes.

First Sailor You want to know?

Second Sailor I do. Tell me.

First Sailor You'll find all this out soon enough.

Second Sailor Tell me.

First Sailor [*looking around to make sure there are no officers in earshot*] I saw the surgeon's mate throw a living slave overboard.

Second Sailor What?

First Sailor You keep that quiet. A slave's money.

Second Sailor What happened?

First Sailor The slave was sick. Shaking about. Eyes rolling back. The surgeon's mate and his helper was trying to get the medicine in him. They couldn't. They was getting angrier and angrier. More and more violent like. And then they just picks him up and they throws him overboard.

Second Sailor Lord! Why did they . . .

First Sailor He was trouble to them. He was work for them. They told the surgeon the slave had died from his illness. I could tell you things that happens on these ships. The owners in Liverpool, they know nothing. Fine houses, fine drinks, fine clothes, fine churches. [*Points down to the grating*] We knows where that comes from. We got them in 'seventy-five.

Second Sailor 'seventy-five?

First Sailor 1775. Year of the Bloody Flag.

Second Sailor What?

First Sailor You not been in Liverpool?

Second Sailor Only got there this year.

First Sailor In 'seventy-five, we marched on those bastards. The merchants. Trying to cut our wages. Look what we do for them. We nearly burnt the Exchange down. Cutting wages? Look how many of us don't come back from these voyages. Voyages of the damned. Either you die or you lose your soul. The bastards. [*Pause*] How come you on this voyage?

Second Sailor I need wages. I want adventure.

First Sailor [*scathingly*] Adventure?

[*Sounds in West African languages emanate from belowdecks*]

Second Sailor [*making a talking motion with his hand*] What you think they jabber about?

First Sailor The Lord knows and I don't care. Damn them.

Second Sailor Jabber, jabber, jabber, jabber.

[*They laugh. The sound of the slaves – their chains clinking – rises from belowdecks*]

First Sailor [*brutally lashing the grating with his whip and shouting into it*] Shut up, you bastards! [*The noise subsides*]

Second Sailor Can we feed this lot all the way to Jamaica?

First Sailor The Captain's stuffed this ship with yams and plantains and Indian corn. There's always enough. [*Shouting into the grating at the unseen slaves*] The problem's with those who won't eat. [*Addressing* **Second Sailor** *again*] Always some o' them.

Second Sailor There's so many of them, so few of us. More than four hundred slaves and just seventeen crew!

First Sailor Don't worry about that.

Second Sailor Does slaves ever rise against the ship?

First Sailor It's happened. I done ten voyages. They rose on one. We'd just left the African coast. That's when it happens. They think they can get back home.

Second Sailor Lord Jesus!

First Sailor You scared?

Second Sailor No.

First Sailor Well, don't be. They's chained and we's not. We's armed and they's not. You never seen the swivel guns do their work? Anyway, when they's up from below, they's chained and we lock them to the deck. [*Pointing down*] That's what these hoops are for. Guns and whips and shackles frees the ship of rebellion. They's guarded and watched all the time. This ship's safe.

Second Sailor Hope so.

First Sailor [*laughing*] The trade takes some getting used to. But there's good things in it.

Second Sailor Not the wages.

First Sailor Not wages. Wenches. The black wenches.

Second Sailor The wenches?

First Sailor You'll learn. They's not all for the Captain.

[*Blackout*

Scene Seven

Kenwood House – the study

[**Mansfield** *at his desk studying Park's manuscript on marine insurance*]

Enter **Dido**

Dido How are your hands, my Lord?

Mansfield They ache. The balms are useless. Only the intricacies of marine insurance distract me from the pain.

Dido The law is your physic, my lord.

[*They laugh*]

Mansfield You've been at the dairy?

Dido Yes, my lord.

Mansfield The countess took such delight in it. [*Pause*] How is Molly?

Dido Sickly. She eats and drinks but little, my lord.

Mansfield That cow was the pride and joy of the countess. More like a treasured pet than a dairy cow. She was always showing off her pedigree.

[*Sounds of a horse. A bell rings*]

Dido I shall see who is here, my lord.

Mansfield Let the footmen.

Dido I am expecting Mr. Davenier.

Mansfield [*disappointed*] Oh.

[*Exit* **Dido**]

Mansfield [*walking slowly towards his wife's portrait*] No children of our own, my love. Just our nieces, Elizabeth and Dido. [*Pause*] My judgements are my progeny. My immortality rests only in the law. [**Mansfield** *walks away from the portrait and sits down, looking once more at Park's manuscript*]

Enter **Dido**, *holding an envelope*

Dido It was not Mr. Davenier, my lord. A missive from the indefatigable Mr. Park. [**Dido** *hands* **Mansfield** *the envelope*]

Mansfield Thank you. I would be alone to consider this.

[*Exit* **Dido**]

Mansfield [*opening the envelope and beginning to read Park's letter aloud*] 'Dear Lord Mansfield, I thank you greatly for the illuminating discourse on your various judgements relating to perils of the sea. Their cogency is compelling. But if I may, my lord, play the devil's advocate . . .' [**Mansfield** *stops reading and looks up*] Hah! Half the barristers who come before me act for the devil. [**Mansfield** *continues reading the letter aloud*] 'Surely the human cargo carries with it certain legal implications of which ordinary cargo is void.' [**Mansfield** *puts the letter down and raises his voice in anger*] No, no.

Enter **Dido**

Dido Did you call my lord?

Mansfield Foolish young man.

Dido Who, my lord?

Mansfield Park.

Dido Such spleen you bear him, my lord!

Mansfield The kidney of this letter!

Dido What has he done?

Mansfield He muddies what I have made clear.

Dido I don't understand.

Mansfield Type of cargo is immaterial to the law.

Dido Oh, marine insurance, again.

Mansfield I will have to set him right. I can't have his volume confusing people. I must write to him again. The tedium of it all.

Dido Tedium, my lord?

Mansfield The tedium of warning people away from anything that would confuse the law and disturb the commerce of this realm. [**Dido** *makes to leave*] Dido.

Dido Yes, my lord.

Mansfield [*tenderly*] Stay with me a while. [**Dido** *sits*] You are expecting Mr. Davenier.

Dido Yes, my lord.

Mansfield He seems to take much interest in you, my dear.

Dido He is a fine man.

Mansfield I am sure. [*Pause*] Dido, when I . . . when I join the countess, you will be free to marry.

Dido Not before, my lord?

Mansfield I have made provision for you. A competence. An annual sum. With that and the £500 your father left to you . . .

Dido I must wait?

Mansfield I will leave you also a capital amount similar to your father's bequest.

Dido I may not marry until you die?

Mansfield What I leave you will allow a suitable marriage.

[*A silence*]

Dido Do you consider me your slave, my lord?

Mansfield What?

Dido Do you consider me your slave?

Mansfield [*sternly*] You will stay with me at Kenwood House until I decide otherwise.

Dido So you do own me, my lord? [**Dido** *waits for* **Mansfield***'s reply*] What is my status under the law, my lord?

Mansfield This is preposterous.

Dido You know the law, my lord. What is my status? I am born to a slave and brought to this country. Am I not a slave under the law?

Mansfield You may leave this room now, Dido. [**Dido** *gets up from the chair but as she is leaving* **Mansfield** *calls out*] Dido. [**She** *continues to leave*] Dido. [**She** *stops and turns*] My dear . . . I should not have spoken harshly. I . . . I am sorry. Stay. Stay with me a while.

Dido [*relenting, she sits down*] My lord.

Mansfield Yes, my dear.

Dido There are people who think I am a slave.

Mansfield They are of no account. I will make it clear to all that you are not.

Dido My mother. [*Pause*] A slave. [*Pause*] My lord, I often wonder what would have become of me had you and the countess not taken me in?

Mansfield But we did.

Dido Yes, my lord, but had you not . . .

Mansfield My dear Dido. There was no question of our not taking you in. You are the child of my neph . . . my late nephew.

Dido He would not take me into his household.

Mansfield That was . . . complicated, my dear.

Dido Yes. Complicated, my lord. Because he was not married to my mother and because she was a slave. [*Pause*] You know, my lord, my father barely saw me all these years and now he is dead.

Mansfield He thought of you, my dear. That is why you are in his will.

Dido Do you see how he refers to me there? His 'reputed daughter.' Reputed. What a euphemism. Never in his English household, never part of his family, and now merely reputed. I feel disowned.

Mansfield Dido!

Dido I am disowned, my lord, because my mother was owned.

Mansfield Do not torture yourself, my dear.

Dido [*pause*] What became of my mother?

Mansfield Your father made arrangements for her.

Dido I know too little of her. I only know that my father was a young officer in the Royal Navy when a Spanish ship was captured, that my mother was part of its *cargo*, that they . . . they became . . . attached to one another. I know I am their child, that he could not be with my mother, that I was born and then that you and the countess took me in. That is all I know, my lord. I don't know what became of my mother. [*Pause*] Is she on a plantation somewhere, my lord?

Mansfield No, Dido, no. Stop this torment.

Dido How could the woman who bore me be tipped off this world, nothing more heard from her or about her? Disappear after giving me life?

Mansfield Dido, my dear, you . . .

Dido Did she want to be separated from me?

Mansfield Dido, Dido.

Dido If my mother was a slave, my lord, am I not a slave?

Mansfield You are not a slave.

Dido But under the law . . . I know something of the law, my lord. I have supped the law in Kenwood House. Half the talk is of the law. I get your casebooks for you. I have read them sometimes. I have taken your correspondence when your hands have been too afflicted. I have heard you practice argument before the mirror. I peruse the folios in the library.

Mansfield [*laughs*] Not those on insurance law, I daresay.

[*Pause*]

Dido [*ignoring Mansfield's attempt at levity*] The law carries all before it in this house. [*Pause*] And it's in the bones of my mother.

Mansfield Dido!

[*Pause*]

Dido The law reached into the bones of my mother.

Mansfield What?

Dido How could the rights of property comprehend a person like that? Encumber the flesh, pass into the bones, claim the breath. [*Pause*] And the children.

Mansfield You are not a slave.

Dido Your books tell me that a slave begets a slave.

Mansfield You are not a slave.

Dido How do I know, my lord?

Mansfield I will show you. [**Mansfield** *opens a drawer in his desk and takes out a document*] This is a copy of my will, Dido. [**Mansfield** *scans it and points at a specific portion*] Here. Read the part pertaining to you. [**Dido** *reads and then slowly looks up*]

Dido It says here that you *confirm* to me my freedom.

Mansfield Yes.

Dido Confirm?

Mansfield This makes clear to all what your status is.

Dido It is written here: 'I confirm to Dido Elizabeth Belle her freedom.'

Mansfield Yes?

Dido Why must this confirmation await your death, my lord? [**Mansfield** *does not answer*] Confirm? Confirm? You confirm something that I have been given? Was freedom bestowed on me at an earlier point, my lord? [**Mansfield** *remains silent*] Then I was a slave and you made me free? [**Mansfield** *is silent*] Why was I not told this, my lord? I am the reputed daughter of my late father, and I am to be confirmed as a free woman on your death. I cannot just be a daughter and be free. [**Dido** *hands the will back to* **Mansfield**] [*Pause*] My lord, will you have anything? [**Mansfield** *remains silent*] My lord.

Mansfield Yes.

Dido Will you have anything, my lord?

Mansfield Oh. Thank you, Dido. Just a little wine, my dear.

Dido I will have a footman bring it. [*Exit* **Dido**

[*Blackout*

Scene Eight

The Zong – the Captain's cabin

Collingwood [*sipping wine, writing his calculations down*] Assuming ten per cent wastage, that will be . . . circa four hundred slaves to Jamaica . . . thirty-five pounds a head . . . fourteen thousand total. My commission on that – seven hundred. Plus monthly salary. Plus five tribute slaves at thirty-five pounds each. I make near a thousand. Near a thousand! [*There is a knock at the door.* **Collingwood** *covers his calculations*] Enter.

Enter **Kelsall**

Collingwood Yes?

Kelsall There is a slave who will not eat, sir.

Collingwood [*anxiously*] For how long?

Kelsall This is the second day. He stares in misery. It is the chagrin.

Collingwood Do his fellows see him?

Kelsall Yes, sir.

Collingwood Apply the cat. Use the *speculum oris*. [*Makes as if turning a screw*] Open the mouth and get the food in him. The others mustn't follow this example. [*Standing up*] Wastage must be kept low on this voyage.

Kelsall Sir.

Collingwood [*pacing around his cabin*] The instruments of this trade. The shackles, the cat, the *speculum oris*, the thumb screw, the swivel gun. None of these prevent the chagrin that seizes hold of so many of the Africans.

Kelsall True, sir. I have been on voyages where the chagrin has crept amongst the slaves like a disease. They refuse to eat, the cat loses its power and they hasten to their deaths as to a blessed release.

Collingwood The physician that can end the chagrin on our ships is a magician.

Kelsall Or an abolitionist. [*They laugh and fall silent*] Sir?

Collingwood What?

Kelsall There is murmuring amongst the slaves, sir.

Collingwood [*startled*] Murmuring?

Kelsall Yes.

Collingwood Murmuring! I know where that leads. Keep them chained and belowdecks? All crew to be vigilant, armed and ready for insurrection.

Kelsall They are.

Collingwood I want the swivel guns manned.

Kelsall They are.

Collingwood Are the women and children confined to their quarters?

Kelsall They are.

Collingwood Good. Of what is the murmuring?

Kelsall Fear of cannibalism.

Collingwood Who told you that?

Kelsall An African who has some English. The slaves believe we ship them to be ate.

Collingwood Where does this rumour come from?

Kelsall I don't know, sir. It recurs in the trade.

Collingwood [*pause*] You know, Kelsall, I was once in Kingston when some of our slaves were put on the quay, before the selling. Some seasoned slaves working at the harbour spoke to them in their language. And all the captives jumped in the water. Most drowned before we could get 'em out. The seasoned slaves had teased them that they were to be ate by the whites.

Kelsall The belief is common. I met a Danish sailor once who told me that a slave thought his black boots were made of Negro skin.

Collingwood The credulity of these folk. They must think us savages.

[Blackout

Scene Nine

The Zong *– sunset on the deck of the slave ship*

  First Sailor *and* **Second Sailor** *emerge, exhausted, from the hatch which leads belowdecks, where the slaves are held.*

[One of the sailors holds a lantern, the other holds the cat o' nine tails]

First Sailor That's the last of them chained for the night.

Second Sailor I've never worked so hard in my life.

First Sailor We's under-crewed. The Captain set off with half the crew we need? Work, work, work. It's all there is. Bring the niggers up to air. Dance them on deck. Clean and smoke the holds. Turf out the shit. Feed the bastards. Take them down for the night. Tend the ship.

Second Sailor I'm sick to death of scraping belowdecks.

First Sailor You can't smoke the stench out of that hell-hole.

Second Sailor Look at my hands. Red and raw. When I scrub belowdecks with vinegar, they burn. They burn!

First Sailor Let me see. [**Second Sailor** *shows him his hands*] Like slave skin scraped by the wood below. Get those seen to. The Captain's a surgeon.

[Blackout

Scene Ten

The Zong *– Captain's cabin.*

[**Collingwood** *asleep on his bed, moaning and crying out in a nightmare. Loud knocking on the door, and calls of 'Sir, sir!'* **Collingwood** *awakes*]

Collingwood Yes?

Kelsall The first mate, sir. Are you all right, sir?

Collingwood Yes. Wait a while. [**Collingwood** *gets up from the bed, lights a lantern and opens the door*] Come in, Kelsall.

Enter **Kelsall**

Kelsall Are you unwell, sir?

Collingwood My sleep is disturbed.

Kelsall I am sorry, sir.

Collingwood The slaves murmur.

Kelsall The murmuring has ceased, sir. They know their fate is sale and labour.

Collingwood I'm sure I heard murmuring below.

Kelsall Captives who dream of home and wake aboard this ship will weep. Sometimes loudly. You hear echoes of that, sir.

Collingwood The men are all chained?

Kelsall Always.

Collingwood Good. When they are brought up to be aired and danced, be sure it is always in small numbers.

Kelsall Of course, sir.

[*They fall silent*]

Collingwood I fear insurrection.

Kelsall We take all precautions, sir, and we are far from the African coast now.

Collingwood [*pause*] Kelsall.

Kelsall Sir.

Collingwood The cargo creeps into my dreams.

Kelsall How do you mean, sir?

Collingwood I dreamed of insurrection.

Kelsall It is a hazard of our trade.

Collingwood I have dreamed of slaves who will not eat or drink, who waste away before our eyes, lost to our enterprise, and cast to the ocean.

Kelsall We have had but few of those upon this voyage.

Collingwood I have dreamt also of the sharks that follow us.

Kelsall Sharks always follow a slaver, sir.

Collingwood Yes.

Kelsall Offal attracts them and also . . . the corpses.

Collingwood How do the sharks *know* to follow us? What do they sense, playing about our ships?

Kelsall We should be grateful, sir. Sometimes they are caught and added to the victuals. They are large fishes.

Collingwood My dreams are strange. The sharks are filled with souls. They swell and then they burst. All are released. A typhoon of souls. They pursue me.

Kelsall A fever dream, sir.

Collingwood Yes. I will read my Bible. This will calm me.

[*Blackout*

Scene Eleven

Kenwood House – the study

[**Mansfield** *at his desk, writing, with difficulty and in pain*]

Enter **Dido**

Dido My lord, you have worked the whole afternoon.

Mansfield Yes. I worry over Park's manuscript. Pages and pages I write to him. [**Mansfield** *holds up his hands and looks at them*] With these useless instruments. [**Mansfield** *continues writing*] Send again to town for a clerk. I must have this copied.

Dido Will you have port, my lord?

Mansfield No. I must finish this letter and I must hear how it sounds. [*Pause*] Have you been at the dairy, Dido?

Dido No, my lord. I have been reading.

Mansfield What?

Dido Sterne.

Mansfield Sterne?

Dido You do not approve?

Mansfield Pah! Trumpery. Which Sterne do you read?

Dido *Tristram Shandy.*

Mansfield This craze for novels, my dear. Sterne and the others, they are all part of this new age of sympathy and romance.

Dido You look askance at sympathy, my lord?

Mansfield It is an enemy of the law. The writers of novels demand that we think ourselves into the skins of others. The law has no skin.

Dido No skin? It does not feel?

Mansfield It is above feeling. It has to be. [*Pause*] I have sacrificed much for the law. Much of myself, much of others, but I have never confused it. How? By guarding it from feeling. [*Pause*] The hulks, the gibbets, the gallows, the prisons – oftentimes, I think on them and how that cruel machinery must be in place for the law to be supreme and protected. I do not set that machinery in motion lightly. Only for the law, and without sentiment. [*Pause*] I will be alone now to finish my letter, if these tortured hands will allow it. [**Mansfield** *begins to write but with evident pain*]

Dido My lord, I will do the writing.

Mansfield No, no, Dido. I will call you if my hands ache too much. I would be alone to read what I have written. Close the door.

[*Exit* **Dido**

Mansfield [*scanning his letter, standing up, and then beginning to read in an authoritative tone, as if speaking before the court*] 'Dear Mr. Park, the *Zong* case came before me twice. In the first case, I found in favour of the traders' insurance claim for slaves thrown overboard. A portion of the cargo was jettisoned, the court believed, in order to save the lives of the crew, the remaining slaves, and to preserve the enterprise as a whole. We saw this as arising from absolute necessity.' [**Mansfield** *stops, sits down, and begins to write with great difficulty. He speaks the words as he writes them*] But – in – a – second – trial . . . [**Mansfield** *stops writing, reflects and then gets up from his desk, walking to his wife's portrait, putting his hand out towards it*] You were still with us, my dear, when I heard the case about which I write. I could draw upon your strength. And look what I faced. Abolitionists! Crawling over the case. A short hand writer following my every word and question. Granville Sharp was there. That man, my God! Gaunt cheeks, angular jaw, and that long inquisitive nose. He would corrupt the law. [**Mansfield**'s *voice rises*] Corrupt the law.

Scene Twelve

The Zong – on deck, by the hatch leading to the slave hold

[**Second Sailor** *in agitation, holding a lamp and a whip*]

Second Sailor [*pacing about, then kneeling*] The flux! The bloody flux! Please God, no. [*Pause*] Not to die on the seas. My body sewn up in sail cloth, weighted, dumped in the ocean, chased by sharks as it plunges past them. Please God. I don't ask for much. Just to die on land, buried in the soil of your good earth, where my people will know where I lie. I don't want my mother to look out at the sea and wonder where I am. Lord Jesus, I . . .

Enter **Collingwood**

[**Second Sailor** *rises*]

Collingwood You been praying?

Second Sailor Yes, sir.

Collingwood [*nodding and gesturing towards the grating*] What did you see down there?

Second Sailor We went down to start bringing the slaves up to air.

Collingwood Well?

Second Sailor [*in agitation*] The flux is taking hold. There's . . . fluid running down there.

Collingwood Are there men belowdecks?

Second Sailor There's hundreds, sir.

Collingwood Not slaves, damn you. Men. Sailors.

Second Sailor There's still four men down there, sir. All armed.

Collingwood Slaves all chained?

Second Sailor Yes, sir.

Collingwood Give me the lamp. [*Opening the hatch to the* *hold he starts to descend*] The stench! [*He briefly disappears then returns, gesturing to the* **Second Sailor**] Give me the cat.

[**Collingwood** *takes the whip and descends into the hold*

Second Sailor [*pacing about, then kneeling in prayer*] Dear Jesus, keep the flux from me. Keep that stinkin,' runnin' mess belowdecks away from me. Oh, God, let me see me Mam again. If you does that for me, I'll . . .

First Sailor *emerges from the hold, overheated, in need of fresh air*

First Sailor Praying again? [**Second Sailor** *rises*] Ain't much use for praying now.

Second Sailor [*in fear*] What you mean? How far we from Jamaica?

First Sailor A month, I'd say.

Second Sailor Does it always take this long?

First Sailor No.

Second Sailor What's happened?

First Sailor The damned calms. We should have been there by now.

Second Sailor The bloody flux, no wind. Like the ship's cursed.

First Sailor With a useless Captain.

Second Sailor What?

First Sailor He don't know the winds and the currents.

Second Sailor Why you say that?

First Sailor I heard him talking to the first mate and the passenger we got in Anomabu.

Second Sailor Mr. Stubbs?

First Sailor Aye.

Second Sailor What they talk about?

First Sailor Captain pretends he's just discussin' things what interest him about the sea.

Second Sailor Pretends?

First Sailor A Captain should know the sea. He tries to get information from 'em. He don't know the sea. If you don't know the sea and you're on it . . . well.

Second Sailor [*nervously*] Yes?

First Sailor The sea finds you out. Plays with you.

Second Sailor Plays with you?

First Sailor It might send a storm. Might stop the wind, like it done to us. Might send sickness to the ship.

Second Sailor The sea ain't God!

First Sailor You ever been at sea in a storm?

Second Sailor No.

First Sailor The sea holds the ship in a giant's hand. Any time it wants, it can tighten into a fist, snap the mast, fill the ship with water, blow men overboard, dash them on the deck. The noise of the storm. You scream to say anything. Nobody can hear you.

Second Sailor Surely, God will . . .

First Sailor He can't hear prayers in a storm.

Second Sailor What will happen to us?

First Sailor The flux will go through the slaves and it will come for us.

Second Sailor Lord!

First Sailor They brought too few of us. We can't clean belowdecks properly. Seventeen crew for four hundred and fifty niggers. We's half what's needed. [*Looking at the hatch*] I better go see what he wants done.

[**First Sailor** *descends*

[**Second Sailor** *paces in increasing agitation; he kneels once more, head bowed, eyes closed. There is a long pause*]

Second Sailor Lord. [*Pause*] No more wenchin,' if that's what you want. Is it what we did to the wenches, Lord, is that why? [*Pause*] The creakin' and the moanin' and the howlin' – sometimes I don't knows whether it be the sea or the slaves or the wind. But it's evil, Lord. This ship's evil. If I can get off it, I can be good. Get me off this ship, my Lord. Please.

First Sailor *emerges from belowdecks*

First Sailor More prayers? Get up. You got work to do.

[**Second Sailor** *stands up*]

First Sailor Captain wants the sickest negroes up. Put 'em in the sick quarters, he says, and also the long boat. Keep them chained.

Second Sailor Can they get well again?

First Sailor If the flux has truly got them, they won't come out alive from the sick quarters. [*Pause*] All right, let's get the other men.

[*Exit* **First Sailor** *and* **Second Sailor**

[*Blackout*

Scene Thirteen

Kenwood House – the study

Enter **Dido**

Dido Did you call, my Lord?

Mansfield No. [**Mansfield** *gestures at the painting before which he stands*] I was speaking to the countess. As is my wont. When she was alive, I consulted the countess always. I cannot break the habit. [*Pause*] Sometimes, I expect the lips to move. They do not. And then there is pain. [**Mansfield** *looks at* **Dido** *and sees a great sadness in her, too*] You are sad also, my dear.

Dido [*pause*] You have a painting of the beloved countess, my lord. I have nothing of my mother. Nothing. Not even a memory.

[**Mansfield** *is unable to respond. He walks back to his desk, picks up his pen and begins to write with a painful slowness. After a while, he puts down the pen, grimacing, and holds his hands claw-like before his eyes*]

Mansfield The pain of writing!

Dido You cannot write in this condition, my lord. [**Mansfield** *ponders*] You cannot write in this condition.

Mansfield You are right, my dear.

Dido You will dictate to me. Give me the letter.

Mansfield No. No. Use clean sheets of paper. You need not trouble yourself with the substance of what comes before.

Dido All right, my lord.

Mansfield A clerk will collate the two sections.

Dido Fine, my lord

[**Mansfield** *gets up, holding the draft of his letter to Park and the letter he has recently received from Park.* **Dido** *sits down at* *the desk and takes a clean sheet of paper.* **Mansfield** *walks up and down, slowly, pondering.* **Dido** *waits, pen in hand*]

Mansfield Write this to Mr. Park. [**Mansfield** *dictates at a slow pace*] 'In the second case relating to the *Zong* . . .'

Dido Ah, my lord, one of Mr Park's quizzically-named ships.

Mansfield [*irritated*] Yes. Let me continue. 'In the second case relating to the *Zong*, new facts came to light, suggesting that insurance might not be claimed on the . . . the . . . the cargo jettisoned.'

Dido What was the cargo, my lord?

Mansfield No matter.

Dido It makes dictation more interesting when I know the subject.

Mansfield Don't trouble yourself about the cargo. I must get this down for the clerk. [**Dido** *shrugs.* **Mansfield** *continues pacing and dictating*] 'The second case is of particular relevance in defining perils of the sea. New facts came to light, and foremost amongst them was this. The ship *Zong* . . .'

Dido [*laughs*] That name again, my lord.

Mansfield What?

Dido That name. Happy as a bell. Ding dong, *Zong*, *Zong*.

Mansfield [*in ill temper*] How can I keep my train of thought if your jocularity intrudes?

Dido Sorry, my lord, but the name of the ship. The *Zong*. How can anyone forget it? [*Laughs*] It will never leave my head.

Mansfield Dido, please.

Dido Sorry, my lord.

Mansfield Where was I?

Dido [*perusing what she has written*] You've said, my lord, that new facts came to light.

Mansfield Ah, yes. [**Mansfield** *paces*] Write thus. 'The voyage of the *Zong*, it turned out, was delayed and struck by catastrophe not through storms or enemy action, but through navigational error of the Captain. His blunder . . .'

Dido Should I call him Captain Blunder, my lord?

Mansfield What?

Dido The Captain's name?

Mansfield Why is that of importance?

Dido [*laughing*] Detail keeps me alert, my lord. You know this.

Mansfield Let us continue.

Dido Yes, my lord.   [*Blackout*

Scene Fourteen

The Zong *– at twilight, on deck*

[*By the hatch leading to the hold;* **Collingwood** *leaning on a stick, weak, mopping his brow intermittently*]

Collingwood I've examined those in sick quarters. On no account must any return belowdecks. Isolate them from the others.

Kelsall Yes, sir.

Collingwood We can arrest the flux to some degree through such measures.

Kelsall What treatment, sir, for those in the sick quarters?

Collingwood I do not expect recovery for most of them.

Kelsall Extra water, sir?

Collingwood For those few who are not too far gone. We can't maintain those who'd arrive in Jamaica as gasping corpses. The buyers won't touch them anyway. I want them overboard as soon as they expire. The longer they are preserved the more they spread the flux. [*Pause*] Our wastage so far is but eighteen?

Kelsall Two more dead this morning, sir, as I informed you.

Collingwood That's twenty. We have a margin then. Our owners will accept ten per cent loss. That's forty-five. Three weeks to Jamaica. We can contain the flux. If it be God's will that another twenty-five be launched into eternity, we can still bring four hundred to market. We must get to market. The wind is with us now. Many days the Lord chose not to fill our sails, but now He does. The flux has found the *Zong* and we must race against it. Separate the ill from the healthful, dispose quickly of the dead. We must scrub and smoke belowdecks more. Use more vinegar.

Kelsall Sir, we are shorthanded. The men are exhausted.

Collingwood God is blowing us toward Jamaica. We will get there soon enough

Kelsall Sir, can we not stop at Barbados for water, physic and refreshment? The men are tired.

Collingwood No, no, absolutely not. The wind blows, we must to market.

[*They fall silent.* **Collingwood** *mops his brow*]

Kelsall Forgive me, sir. You look unwell.

Collingwood It's something I picked up on the African coast. I sweat fiercely and shiver. Sometimes I shake. Like a ship in violent storm. Rum is my relief. [**Collingwood** *looks closely at* **Kelsall**] You too look unwell.

Kelsall I feel weak.

[*Blackout*

Scene Fifteen

The Zong – at dawn

[*Entrance to slave hold where* **First Sailor** *and* **Second Sailor** *are standing by the grating*]

First Sailor What a picture of hell belowdecks! The moans and the stench. Every day more dead. One in seven of the slaves be dead now.

Second Sailor And the crew sickens. Half of us can do no work.

First Sailor I'm sick even of dancing them on deck.

[*They fall silent*]

Second Sailor [*despairingly*] You think we'll get back home?

First Sailor [*looking around to make sure there are no officers in earshot*] If we do, it won't be by the Captain. Why give us a surgeon for a Captain? Leaving Africa short-crewed and overstocked with cargo.

Second Sailor So tight-packed down there. It's hard to move amongst them. Like treading flesh.

First Sailor [*pause*] I long for home. [*Pause*] We're sailing a coffin.

[*Blackout*

Scene Sixteen

The Zong – dawn on deck of the slave ship

[**Collingwood** *and* **Kelsall**, *both unwell*]

Collingwood We'll have them up to air soon?

Kelsall Yes, sir. [*Suddenly pointing*] Look! Land.

Collingwood Good Lord! [**Collingwood** *looks through a telescope*] Hispaniola. That's Hispaniola.

Kelsall Not Jamaica, sir?

Collingwood No, Hispaniola.

Kelsall Are you sure, sir?

Collingwood [*looking through the telescope again*] Hispaniola lies before Jamaica. It must be Hispaniola. We're sure to strike Jamaica soon. This wind will blow us there in no time.

Kelsall If that's Jamaica and we pass it now, we'll face the winds and currents of Hell to get this ship back to the island.

Collingwood [*angrily*] I say we see Hispaniola and not Jamaica!

Kelsall But . . . [*He falls silent in the face of* **Collingwood**'s *authority*] Sixty dead so far, sir.

Collingwood We'll have the rest to market soon. We've done well. The flux could have swept off more.

Kelsall Many of them have the flux, sir.

Collingwood When we make landfall, we'll sell the healthful and wait to revive as many of the others as we can. There's profit still to be had. Our aim must be to minimise refuse. With proper care we can make a good number well again for sale.

Kelsall We make landfall none too soon. The crew murmurs about being shorthanded. Some are painful sick. Others worn from work.

Collingwood The crew that have the flux must be given as much water as they need. Use up all our rum if that makes them happier.

Kelsall There's only rum for us now, sir.

Collingwood We'll be in Jamaica soon. Tell the crew. I must lie down. [**Collingwood** *walks away unsteadily*]

[*Blackout*]

Scene Seventeen

Kenwood House – the study

Mansfield [*pondering and pacing while dictating to* **Dido**] Write thus. 'Errors of crew or captain do not constitute perils of the sea. These are not acts of God. They are stupidities of mankind, which foresight and a proper training would prevent. A contract of insurance cannot cover such.'

Dido A little more slowly, my lord.

Mansfield Sorry. [**Mansfield** *paces silently, then raises his hand, pointing his forefinger authoritatively*] Conclude thus. 'Had there been a peril of the sea, a claim for the jettisoned cargo would have had success.'

Dido Jettison, my lord? What was cast overboard?

Mansfield The sl . . . Dido! The cargo was jettisoned.

Dido But what was the cargo?

Mansfield [*pause*] It is of no import with regard to the legal principle. Let me continue.

Dido Yes, my lord.

[**Mansfield** *paces and thinks*]

Mansfield [*stopping to look at Park's letter*] 'When you write that . . .' [**Mansfield** *looks again at the letter from* **Park**] Dido, the remainder of my letter I will write.

Dido But your hands, my lord, they . . .

Mansfield My dear, leave me now. The matter becomes exceeding technical and I need to think it through. Please. [**Mansfield** *looks again at the letter from* Park. **Dido** *gets up from the desk and leaves the room*]

[*Exit* **Dido**

[**Mansfield** *sits, holding the letter from Park*]

A Peril of the Sea

Mansfield You write [*imitates an earnest, young lawyer*] 'The transaction shocks, my lord! How could they drown them and then claim for those they killed? Surely, my lord, murder cannot be the basis for an insurance claim.' [**Mansfield** *looks up angrily from the letter*] Damn you, young Park, you have much to learn. The case before me was not one of murder. It was one of insurance. I had no business considering it on any other basis. To have done so would have sown confusion. [**Mansfield** *raises his voice*] I will not have that.

[**Dido** *knocks at the door*]

Enter **Dido**

Dido [*concerned*] My lord, what is wrong?

Mansfield This young man has thrown me into agitation.

Dido Again? My lord, he worships you and . . .

Mansfield He tests me.

Dido He will amend his manuscript according to your advice. They always do.

Mansfield [*angrily*] When I have established principles of the law, I will not have them tampered with. Those engaged in trade must know where they stand.

Dido My lord, your health is tried by this. This should be for you a time of repose. The countess would have counselled that you stop your work with the scholars.

Mansfield Who else will protect what I have built?

Dido [*pause*] Your supper awaits you. Put the correspondence away. Work on it tomorrow.

Mansfield Yes, I suppose you are right. [**Mansfield** *puts Park's letter and his draft reply at the back of a pile of correspondence with Park. He places the pile on a corner of his desk, partly protruding over the edge*] I must finish the letter and have it copied. [*Laughs*] The clerk's handwriting is much better than my own, but then he doesn't have my rheumatism.

Dido I have made the arrangements for the clerk.

Mansfield Good. I shall invite Mr. Park for dinner next week to discuss his manuscript and I want to study all this [*gestures at the correspondence*] in preparation. Mr. Park is able but he needs guidance on certain points of law. [*Pause*] Well, to supper. Will you join me, Dido?

Dido It is too early for me, my lord. I must attend to matters at the dairy.

Mansfield Good. [**Mansfield** *begins to leave*]

Dido My lord.

Mansfield Yes.

Dido [*points to books resting on the desk*] Would you have me return these to the library?

Mansfield Please. [*Exit* **Mansfield**

[**Dido** *picks up the volumes from the desk, and makes to leave but, as she does so, she brushes against the pile of correspondence with Park that protrudes over a corner of the desk. The pile falls to the floor*]

Dido Damnation! All jumbled. [**Dido** *picks up the correspondence and begins to order it. As she does so, its subject matter becomes clear to her. She begins reading, aghast*]

[*Blackout*

Scene Eighteen

The Zong *– Captain's cabin*

[**Collingwood** *is poring over a map in agitation, drinking rum, wiping sweat from his face. There is a knock at the door*]

Collingwood Kelsall, is that you?

Kelsall [*offstage*] Yes, sir.

Collingwood Come in.

Enter **Kelsall**

Kelsall You called for me, sir.

Collingwood We should have struck Jamaica by now.

Kelsall I fear that . . . that what you . . . what we called Hispaniola was Jamaica. We have passed the island.

Collingwood Well, let's turn back.

Kelsall We would have to fight the current, sir.

Collingwood Why has God done this to us?

Kelsall We could press on for Spanish America, sir.

Collingwood Jamaica is our market and we must make for it. How long to the island?

Kelsall I don't know, sir. Weeks. We would be fighting the sea the whole way. Our provisions are . . .

Collingwood How much water have we? Have the puncheons checked.

Kelsall We have hundreds that need water aboard this ship, sir, and we are some weeks beyond the usual voyage. The puncheons will be . . .

Collingwood Measure the puncheons.

Kelsall Sir, they will show . . .

Collingwood [*shouting*] I say measure the water!

Kelsall Sir. [*Exit* **Kelsall**

Collingwood [*looking up as if appealing to the heavens*] Lord, I gave my life to physic, to healing. Many times have I restrained the cat when my captains had the wretches lashed. Many times have I brought back to health slaves to whom You directed Your mercy. I have been Your agent. I have prayed for the safe deliverance of our voyage and our cargo. I accepted the calms. I accepted the flux when it seized our ship. I have accepted my fever. I have not lost faith. But to overshoot Jamaica, to have to sail against the way the ocean streams, with dysentery on the ship. What a test is this, oh Lord!

[*Blackout*

Scene Nineteen

The Zong – *Captain's cabin*

[**Collingwood** *seated at a table, head in hands. There is a knock at the door*]

Collingwood [*raising his head*] Yes.

Enter **Kelsall**

Kelsall We have checked the water, sir.

Collingwood [*anxiously*] Well?

Kelsall It would have sufficed with spare had we not mistook Jamaica.

Collingwood How much water is there?

Kelsall About three puncheons sweet, sir.

Collingwood *About* three?

Kelsall They have leaked some inches out.

Collingwood Sour water?

Kelsall There is some rain water stinking in casks that held rum.

Collingwood How much?

Kelsall Two-and-a half casks' worth.

Collingwood [*in panic*] Only?

Kelsall What to do, sir?

Collingwood [*getting up unsteadily*] How quickly could we reach Jamaica?

Kelsall We are lost, sir, and the current is against us.

Collingwood How long will the water last?

Kelsall At full ration, a few days. If we put all to half allowance, we could carry on to America with the wind behind us.

Collingwood If we go there, we may get water but we lose our slaves, our ship and our liberty to the Spanish. [*Pleading*] How can I tell the crew that they may never again see their families or their homeland? Can we not put in to the Caymans or the Isle of Pines?

Kelsall But we be lost, sir. We cannot be sure we will strike them.

[**Collingwood** *looks at the map, remaining silent*]

Collingwood Kelsall, I don't know where we are. I'm a surgeon. I know my way around the human body. Stretches of water are oft a mystery to me.

Kelsall We need the passenger Stubbs, sir. The sea is in his bones. He can guide us.

Collingwood It's weeks to Jamaica, and we have a few days of water. What do I tell the crew?

Kelsall They suspect we've missed the island, sir. The spirit is sullen, mutinous. Beware sailors who have nothing to lose. [*Pauses*] Should we put the men to short allowance?

Collingwood No, no. That's the road to mutiny. [**Collingwood** *falls silent and then speaks as if before a revelation*] I can show them how much I value them. Yes. Yes. I can act for them. I can give them all.

Kelsall What?

Collingwood We have enough water for a few days?

Kelsall Yes.

Collingwood But we waste most of it on the cargo.

Kelsall The slaves?

Collingwood The men will forgive my error if I keep them alive. To give them life, we must take life. How many slaves have the flux?

Kelsall More than a hundred.

Collingwood If we can dispose of a goodly number, we will free water for the crew. There will be no talk of mutiny. They will see that the Captain, even at the cost of the cargo, will do all he can to protect them.

Kelsall Sir, let us make for America.

Collingwood And lose the cargo? To be prisoners of the Spanish? To lose our reputations in Liverpool? No, no. Large numbers of slaves aboard this ship are gripped by the flux. We could have revived them, and sold them, if we put into Jamaica soon. But we can't do that. The choice for them is quick or slow death. I might not know the winds and the currents, but I know the flux. I know the flux. We can rid the sufferers of their agonies, purge the ship of the contagion, use the water to preserve the crew and the remaining slaves.

Kelsall Sir!

Collingwood What do you propose then, Kelsall? Draw lots to see who has rights to water? Divide it all equally? This is not a ship of the Royal Navy. This is a slaver. Call Stubbs.

Kelsall Yes, sir.   [*Exit* **Kelsall**

Collingwood Guidance, my Lord, guidance, I beg you.

[**Collingwood** *paces while he waits for Stubbs. There is a knock at the door*]

Collingwood Yes

Enter **Kelsall**

Kelsall Mr. Stubbs will be with you in fifteen minutes, sir.

Collingwood Fifteen minutes?

Kelsall He shaves, sir.

Collingwood Did you tell him of our situation?

Kelsall I did, sir?

Collingwood What does he say? [**Kelsall** *remains silent.* **Collingwood** *raises his voice*] What does he say?

Kelsall He says, sir, that surgeons should not steer ships.

Collingwood The impudence!

Kelsall Sir, he will help us but . . .

Collingwood What?

Kelsall Sir, he says he is a passenger and not under your command.

Collingwood Not under my command?

Kelsall He is not part of the crew, sir, but we need him.

[**Collingwood**, *angry, nevertheless conceding the point through gesture*]

Collingwood [*pouring himself a drink*] Would you have rum, Kelsall?

Kelsall Thank you, sir.

[*Rum is poured for* **Kelsall**]

Collingwood How could we have missed Jamaica?

Kelsall We did not miss Jamaica, sir. We saw Jamaica and you called it Hispaniola.

[*They drink in silence*]

Collingwood Where is this damned Stubbs? [*Pause*] Have you ever been lost in the ocean before, Kelsall?

Kelsall No, sir.

Collingwood It must be God's will.

Kelsall His will?

Collingwood The Lord has lost this vessel and he drives my decision. I want this ship turned now.

Kelsall You can turn the ship, sir, but the current is against us.

Collingwood If we turn, how long to Jamaica?

Kelsall Stubbs says perhaps three weeks, sir, but we have insufficient provisions. This ship is doomed.

Collingwood I can save the crew.

[*Pause*]

Kelsall When I was at Cape Castle, I heard of a drifting ship come upon by a privateer. Nobody was on board. No crew. No slaves. No sails. The threads of rigging looked liked a ribcage . . .

Collingwood I can save the crew. Those souls I can save.

Kelsall Sir, let us first discuss the situation with Mr. Stubbs.

Collingwood No. The crew before the negroes.

Kelsall You would leave the slaves to die of want of meat and drink?

Collingwood Sixty of them have already died. Double that number now waste from illness. Why wait for them to die starved and parched?

Kelsall Murder?

Collingwood This is not murder. The Lord has called them forth. Why has He taken them from Africa, cast the flux upon them, sped our ship beyond Jamaica, made the current flow against them now? It is the Lord's will. By God, I am a surgeon, and if I could make these wretches well, I would do so. The Lord licenses our trade and tests us by its extremities. I will save this crew. I will call the men together and make the proposition.

Kelsall Mr. Stubbs won't be part of this, sir. He is a passenger.

Collingwood [*with bitter sarcasm*] I trust then, Kelsall, that he will share his allowance of water and food with the slaves. Get all the men on deck. Now.

[*Exit* **Kelsall**

[*Blackout*

Scene Twenty

The Zong – *Captain's cabin*

[*Sounds of a storm.* **Collingwood** *is very ill, feverish. There is a knock at the door*]

Collingwood Yes.

Enter **Kelsall**

Kelsall Sir, the rains lash us and don't stop.

Collingwood I hear.

Kelsall The butts are being refilled.

Collingwood I thank God.

Kelsall The puncheons overflow, sir.

Collingwood Kelsall, God has rewarded us. We've done no wrong.

Kelsall Sir?

Collingwood The throwing overboard. If this was wrong God would have withheld the rains. It is a sign, a sign. We do what is right.

Kelsall We stop the . . . the throwing overboard now?

Collingwood There are still others in the grip of the flux.

Kelsall We have water now, sir.

Collingwood For how long? And food? [**Kelsall** *does not reply*] More must go.

Scene Twenty-One

Kenwood House – the study

[**Mansfield** *at his desk*]

Enter **Dido**

Dido What time will you dine this evening, my lord?

Mansfield The usual time. [**Dido** *nods and makes to leave*] Dido.

Dido Yes, my lord.

Mansfield Your spirits have been uncommon low these past days. Have you been reading those select committee reports again?

Dido No, my lord.

Mansfield I should not have them sent here.

Dido I have not been reading them. [*Pause*] Do you require anything, my lord?

Mansfield No

Dido I shall go then.

Mansfield Will you dine with me tonight?

Dido No, my lord. [**Dido** *begins to leave*]

Mansfield Dido.

Dido Yes, my lord.

Mansfield Last night and the night before, you didn't dine with me because you were ill and resting. What is it tonight? Are you feeling unwell again?

Dido No, my lord.

Mansfield What then? [**Dido** *remains silent*] What is it?

Dido I have had a shock.

Mansfield A shock?

Dido Yes, my lord, a shock.

Mansfield Is this to do with Mr. Davenier?

Dido No, my lord.

Mansfield I will not have that man upsetting you.

Dido It is nothing to do with Mr. Davenier.

Mansfield Oh. What has occasioned the shock?

Dido I prefer not to say, my lord.

Mansfield You will not tell me?

Dido I prefer not to discuss it now, my lord. [*Pause*] May I go, my lord?

Mansfield Yes

[*Exit* **Dido**]

[**Mansfield** *returns to his work at his desk*]

[*Blackout*]

Scene Twenty-Two

The Zong *– on deck*

[*The sailors are closing and sealing the grating leading down to the hold*]

Second Sailor Strange how the rains came.

First Sailor Days and days of rain. Never seen it like that. The puncheons are straining with the water.

Second Sailor The Captain says it's a sign from God.

First Sailor What? God's crying?

Second Sailor Captain says God saved us. That what we done was right, so He sent the rains.

First Sailor In this trade, you does what you does.

Second Sailor I believe in God.

First Sailor This voyage is cursed.

[*They fall silent*]

Second Sailor I can't get some of what we done out my head.

First Sailor You wanted adventure.

Second Sailor Pushing the sick children out the windows like that. The crying. The struggling in the water.

First Sailor You need rum. We all need rum.

[*Pause*]

Second Sailor Are they all heathens?

First Sailor What?

Second Sailor All the slaves. They all heathens?

First Sailor Suppose so.

Second Sailor You think that's why God done it?

First Sailor Done what?

Second Sailor Drowned them?

First Sailor You think Jesus came down from his cross, got on board this ship, and threw them overboard? You mad?

Second Sailor It must have happened for some reason.

First Sailor The trade. But don't worry. Our masters in Liverpool will find a way to squeeze some profit from it. [*Pause*] Even I sometimes . . . [*Pause*]

Second Sailor What?

First Sailor Sometimes lying in my hammock, the sick slaves below me in the long boat, with the stars in the sky, and the sound of the sea all around . . .

Second Sailor Yes?

First Sailor I thinks on it all. The strangeness. The slaves stuffed in the hold. The dead fed to the sharks. The merchants dining and praying in Liverpool. And us sailing and guarding and feeding and shaving and dancing and whipping them. And now killing them. All for wages. Low wages. And then we die. [*Pause*] The Devil's work.

Second Sailor I go to church. I pray. The Captain has us pray twice a day.

First Sailor Didn't help us. Lost our way to Jamaica. [*Pause*] Less praying, more navigation.

[*Blackout*

Scene Twenty-Three

Kenwood House – the study

Enter **Mansfield**, *in great anger, clutching a document*

Mansfield [*shouting*] Dido! Dido!

Enter **Dido**

Mansfield [*handing the document to her*] What is this?

Dido A receipt from the butcher, my lord.

Mansfield For what? I have been to the dairy and I cannot find Molly.

Dido The receipt is for Molly, my lord.

Mansfield Yes?

Dido She has been slaughtered and disposed of.

Mansfield Slaughtered and disposed of? You would have Molly disposed of without consulting me?

Dido I am the superintendent of the dairy, my lord. If I'd waited any longer we would have got nothing for her.

Mansfield Nothing for her! That was the countess's favourite cow.

Dido She was old and declining fast, my lord. She could barely get up. We could not have moved her to market?

Mansfield To market?

Dido Forgive me, my lord, but if one eats beef and runs a dairy one cannot be sentimental about a cow.

Mansfield Sentimental?

Dido You keep warning me about sentiment, my lord.

Mansfield What?

Dido You seem well able to ward away sympathy when your work requires it.

Mansfield How dare you raise your voice to me.

Dido [*placing her hand on the pile of correspondence between Park and* **Mansfield** *that lies on the desk*] I am familiar with this, my lord.

Mansfield What?

Dido I have read this correspondence.

Mansfield You would read my correspondence?

Dido It fell and scattered, my lord. I had to order it. It is in order now. Everything is clear.

Mansfield You would read my correspondence with Mr. Park about matters of insurance?

Dido Insurance? This is not about insurance. This is about murder and you have justified it.

[*A brief silence*]

[**Mansfield**'s *tone changes from anger to one of pleading*]

Mansfield Dido, Dido. This came to me as an insurance case concerning jettisoned cargo.

Dido Am I cargo?

Mansfield No, Dido. No, dear Dido.

Dido My mother was a slave. Was she cargo? Cargo begets cargo.

Mansfield The case came to me as one of jettison.

Dido It is murder, and you call it jettison.

Mansfield It was brought to me as a matter of insurance claimed on jettisoned car . . .

Dido [*shouting*] People.

Mansfield Dido, you must understand my position as Lord Chief Justice.

Dido We have discussed the law. You have always told me that murder is never justified unless against one who attacks you and puts you in mortal danger.

Mansfield The crew were in danger of dying of thirst.

Dido Who had put them in that danger? The slaves murdered were not trying to kill them.

Mansfield Dido!

[**Dido** *picks up the correspondence and slams it down on the table; she is shaking*]

Dido [*clutching her hand and showing it to* **Mansfield**] What makes this property? What guts it of all other meaning? You!

Mansfield Dido, Dido . . . please. I am bound to protect and nourish legal principle.

Dido What principle?

Mansfield Necessity. Jettison. Perils of the Sea.

Dido Whatever they are, they lie on a thick raft of corpses.

[**Mansfield** *reaches for* **Dido** *but she avoids his touch*]

Mansfield My dear, you speak as if I killed those slaves.

Dido You denied that they were murdered.

Mansfield It came to me as a case of insurance.

Dido Why did you not send it to the Attorney-General as a case of murder?

Mansfield Please, Dido, understand. There is law regarding cargo and I had to apply it when considering that case . . .

Dido Cargo? Can you not see anything beyond property?

Mansfield The law of insurance requires me . . .

Dido This is the law that *you* have built through *your* judgments and you allow nothing, not even massacre, nor yet the law against murder, to shake it. And for what?

Mansfield Dido, please . . .

Dido For trade. What alchemy you perform, my lord? Truly, a magician. You fuse the people with the cargo, cast your spell, and the people disappear. [**Dido** *turns and begins to leave*]

Mansfield Dido, Dido.

[**Dido** *stops, and slowly returns to* **Lord Mansfield**. *She still holds the receipt that he had asked her about at the beginning of the scene*]

Dido [*holding the receipt out to him*] Your receipt, my lord.

Mansfield What?

Dido For the butchery.

[*Blackout*

Afterword

My play deals with the world of the slave ship *Zong*, which I have explored as a historian, and I am bound to say something about how my play relates to history.

In 1781, the *Zong* left West Africa with over 450 slaves on board, and it succumbed to an ordinary and then an extraordinary tragedy of the slave trade. First, there was the ordinary tragedy. Around sixty slaves died from unspecified causes, no doubt relating to the conditions in which they were held: epidemics of dysentery, for example, were common on slave ships. And then, there was the extraordinary tragedy: through navigational error of the Captain, the ship passed its destination, Jamaica, and when the error was realised, it was found that regaining that island would take weeks but that there were only a few days of water supplies left. The fateful decision was then taken to throw slaves overboard – this continued day after day, even after rains began to fall and replenish water supplies – so that around 130 slaves were killed in this way.[1] The ship ultimately made its way back to Jamaica, and this might simply have been an unknown tragedy of the slave trade had not the owners of the ship decided to claim insurance on the slaves killed. This set the stage for a battle between the slave traders and the insurers, one that found its way to court.

The insurance claim, adjudicated by the Chief Justice, Lord Mansfield, was initially upheld on the grounds of 'necessity' – that is, that under marine insurance law, it was permitted in the case of unforeseen and unavoidable emergency to jettison cargo and claim for it if this was undertaken to preserve a voyage from disaster. The first

---

1 Strictly speaking, some of these slaves – a very small minority – threw themselves into the sea (rather than being thrown in) as the crew's murderous intent became clear to them. Perhaps they sought to avoid being shackled before being cast overboard.

case, then, was decided in favour of the slave traders. But those who had insured the ship pursued the matter and a second trial took place. That trial suggested that the error of the captain in passing Jamaica was the likely cause of the ship's catastrophic water shortage, and it called the initial judgement into question. The emergency, it seemed, had not resulted from some unforeseeable 'peril of the sea' (for example, a storm that delayed the voyage) so it was questionable if a claim for insurance could be made on the 'cargo' thrown overboard. Moreover, it was held, the fact that the killing continued even after the rains had resupplied the ship with water weakened the case of those claiming insurance on the murdered slaves. A further trial was therefore allowed, but it never took place. The owners of the *Zong* ceased to press their claim: they had lost confidence, one imagines, because of the questions raised by the court in the second case and because abolitionists were now taking up the cause of the slaves who were drowned.

The scholarly articles that I have written on the *Zong* explore two facets of it: first, the terrible events that unfolded on board the ship in 1781; and, second, the legal judgement and logic that – in effect – refused to consider the slaves as victims of murder and left them as 'cargo,' the subjects of an insurance claim.[2] *A Peril of the Sea* is a theatrical imagining of the issues at play as well as an attempt to evoke in drama a history that can never fully be retrieved. This play is, of course, a work of fiction but it is also a work of the historical imagination, one fired by many years of research and thought about the *Zong*. To a considerable degree, my rendering of the world of the slave ship and the slave trade is rooted in

---

[2] See Jeremy Krikler, 'A Chain of Murder in the Slave Trade: A Wider Context of the *Zong* Massacre' *International Review of Social History*, 57 (2012) and Jeremy Krikler, 'The *Zong* and the Lord Chief Justice' *History Workshop Journal*, 64 (2007).

A Peril of the Sea

evidence of the eighteenth century slave trade – much of it can be followed in sources cited in my historical articles. Likewise, my rendering of the legal logic and evasions of Lord Chief Justice Mansfield, though rendered in dramatic form, was explored first through my historical research.

I have sought in this play to remain true to the historical phenomena that are its subject. I must note, however, certain conscious departures from the historical record necessitated by the demands of writing a play. They relate to the characters Park and Dido. James Park, a young barrister and legal scholar, interacted with Lord Mansfield and took advice from him with regard to the book on marine insurance law that he wrote and in which the *Zong* figures.[3] While the play absorbs this into the drama, there is no evidence of Park challenging Mansfield (much to the Lord Chief Justice's irritation) as he does in the play. This was a device used to force upon the character Mansfield (and convey to the audience) the fact that the Lord Chief Justice ignored the law against murder when he considered the *Zong* case.

The character Dido, who is much more central to the play than is Park, reflects in some ways what is known of Dido Elizabeth Belle. She was the niece of Lord Mansfield and was the daughter of a slave by Mansfield's nephew; she lived with Mansfield and occupied the curious position of both privileged servant and (second class) family member; she oversaw the dairy at Kenwood House, Mansfield's Hampstead estate; and she sometimes assisted him in his correspondence.[4]

---

[3] I sketch the relationship between Park and Mansfield in my 'The *Zong* and the Lord Chief Justice.'

[4] Again, Dido's place in Mansfield's household/family is traced in my article, 'The *Zong* and the Lord Chief Justice' which details the sources I used to reconstruct how they related to one another.

All of this is reflected in the play. But in *A Peril of the Sea*, it is Dido's challenging Lord Mansfield on questions of slavery and the law, and her confrontation with him on his role in the case of the *Zong*, that emphasise the immorality and evasions (including of the law) that lie at the heart of his role in the *Zong* case. This is not something the historical Dido did. All the evidence we have of her suggests a very great deference to Lord Mansfield, and – notwithstanding their closeness – a complete subordination to him and his needs. In this play, she becomes the black abolitionist voice of the late-eighteenth century. But she could only do this, and thereby illuminate fully some of the play's key historical and ethical issues, if she parted company with the actual Dido.